AMERICA'S
TWELVE GREAT
WOMEN LEADERS

AMERICA'S
TWELVE GREAT

WOMEN LEADERS

DURING THE
PAST HUNDRED YEARS

AS CHOSEN
BY THE WOMEN
OF AMERICA

•

A Compilation from
THE LADIES' HOME JOURNAL
and
THE CHRISTIAN SCIENCE
MONITOR

Essay Index Reprint Series

BOOKS FOR LIBRARIES PRESS
FREEPORT, NEW YORK

First Published 1933
Reprinted 1969

STANDARD BOOK NUMBER:
8369-1202-0

LIBRARY OF CONGRESS CATALOG CARD NUMBER:
74-90600

PRINTED IN THE UNITED STATES OF AMERICA

FOREWORD
AND ACKNOWLEDGMENTS
TO ORIGINAL EDITION

Occupying a prominent place in the exhibit of the National Council of Women in the Hall of Social Science at A Century of Progress, in Chicago, during 1933, are portraits of twelve women recently chosen by the women of America in a nation-wide poll as the great women leaders of the past century. It seems fitting that there should be made available a statement of the method whereby the women thus honored were chosen. Also, there should be preserved in permanent form the timely material published at the time of the selection. This booklet is designed to fulfill that two-fold purpose.

To The Curtis Publishing Company is tendered thanks for permission to use material contained in its announcement in the November, 1932, issue of The Ladies' Home Journal as a basis for the contents of pages 6 and 7 of this booklet, also for permission to reprint on pages 50 to 55 of this booklet, the editorial comment and the prize winning letters as originally published in the April, 1933, number of The Ladies' Home Journal.

The publishers also acknowledge with thanks the permission of The Christian Science Monitor to reproduce from its issues of January 16, 1933 to January 28, 1933, the biographical sketches of the Twelve Women Leaders of the past hundred years.

WHEN IS A WOMAN A LEADER?

"WHAT twelve women have made the most valuable contribution to American progress during the past hundred years?" To answer that question The Ladies' Home Journal announced, in its issue of November, 1932, a poll of the women of America.

Sponsor of the poll, in conjunction with The Ladies' Home Journal, was the National Council of Women, an affiliation of thirty-one women's organizations. As part of its exhibit at A Century of Progress, in Chicago, in 1933, it was planned to give prominent place to portraits of the twelve great women leaders of the century. A frieze consisting of silhouettes of twelve women who had exercised a distinct influence upon the life of the century had been chosen for the letterhead of the council.

"But," it was asked, "are these the twelve most outstanding women leaders of the past hundred years? Could others be chosen who have still greater claim to recognition?" Through the pages of The Ladies' Home Journal the question was thrown open to all the women of the nation.

At the same time, awards were offered for the four best 300 word letters on "The Essential Qualities of the Woman Leader."

As Miss Lena Madesin Phillips, president of the National Council of Women, said in announcing the results of the poll at a dinner given at the Hotel Vanderbilt on December 20, 1932, "We believe that civilization cannot progress much beyond the ideas and ideals of mankind. Therefore it is important to bring out into the open the qualities of real leadership which are of lasting value."

The following three questions were offered as a test to be applied in measuring great leaderships:

1. Has she intellectual, moral or spiritual qualities which raise her above her fellows?

2. Has she to her credit an achievement so outstanding as to entitle her to individual recognition?

3. Is that achievement so important as to have affected definitely her times?

By the end of the time allotted, 128,882 ballots were received by The Ladies' Home Journal. On the next following pages of this booklet are reprinted from The Christian Science Monitor, January 16 to January 28, 1933, biographical sketches of the twelve great women leaders of the past hundred years as chosen by the women of America.

The illustrations are by Dwight C. Sturges (staff artist of The Christian Science Monitor) a nationally known etcher, member of the American Society of Etchers and other organizations, and winner of many awards. Specimens of Mr. Sturges' work are included in many of the principal art museums of the country.

ROLL OF HONOR

Here is the list of winners in the poll for America's twelve great women leaders, with the names arranged alphabetically and with the number of votes that were given to each.

•

JANE ADDAMS
Founder of Hull House in Chicago · 99,147

SUSAN B. ANTHONY
Woman Suffrage Leader · 84,321

CLARA BARTON
Founder of the Red Cross · 96,139

CARRIE CHAPMAN CATT
Suffrage Leader · 70,489

MARY BAKER EDDY
Founder of the Christian Science Church · 102,762

JULIA WARD HOWE
Composer of the "Battle Hymn of the Republic" · 72,276

HELEN KELLER
Deaf and Blind Lecturer · 84,239

MARY LYON
Founder of Mount Holyoke College · 40,831

AMELIA EARHART PUTNAM
43,399

HARRIET BEECHER STOWE
Author of "Uncle Tom's Cabin" · 73,999

FRANCES E. WILLARD
Founder of the Woman's Christian Temperance Union
90,303

DR. MARY E. WOOLLEY
President of Mount Holyoke College and Delegate to the Geneva Disarmament Conference · 36,855

JANE ADDAMS

*Hull House Founded as Haven of Cheer
for Lonely People*

WHEN the Chicago fire swept the neighborhood of Halsted and Polk Streets in 1871, the mansion of Charles Hull, wealthy farmer and landowner, was saved. Eighteen years later Ellen Gates

Starr and Jane Addams were looking for a base for "neighboring" with immigrants of two-score nations who were floundering around in a strange land trying to find work and freedom. Seeing the Charles Hull mansion, they said, "God's hand must have saved this for us," took it over and established Hull House which has become a sort of beacon for the whole settlement movement.

Jane Addams was born of Quaker parents and she spent a lonely childhood because her mother passed on when she was quite small. Perhaps the things she missed having done for her, the companionship, the touches that humanize living, filled Jane Addams early with the yearning wish to do things for other lonely people. John Addams, her father, was a banker-miller; he was a member of the Assembly, and a close friend of Abraham Lincoln and he had perhaps neither the time nor the exact insight to fill in the gaps in the rearing of his motherless child.

When Hull House became established it was Miss Addams' custom sometimes to look back at the impulses in her that had contributed to it. She used to go to her father's mill as a child, and all about it were dirty tenements, and ragged people, and squalor and unhappiness. "I knew that when I grew up," she said, "I would have a large home, but not one among other large homes; no, a large home right in the midst of small, dirty homes and the people from those homes would come over to mine."

Like many another social worker Miss Addams took inspiration from Toynbee Hall in London. She and Miss Starr spent many hours there, when they were feeling their way into the future, searching for just the idea they wanted to crystallize.

When Hull House was first opened the neighbors didn't know what to think. They came to it gingerly. Then in greater numbers. They heard English spoken there, and experimented with it. They remembered handicraft which was synonymous with their own, far-off homes, and found they could revive their skill at it in Hull House. They found Jane Addams there, a plain, stalwart, simple woman, who smiled genially at them, and found out things that were distressing them, and helped them to put them right.

Hull House grew, wandering over partitions and across little alleys until now it is a sort of architectural nest, with all kinds of additions, both of wood and plaster and of idea. Many things in the social service history of the United States, and even of the world, have their roots down in Hull House.

If you asked Miss Addams to tell you the story of Hull House she would probably smile slightly and say it was just a matter of having done one thing at a time. In the beginning a simple plan, but one that would grow. And it grew and grew. Interest in foreign-born people moving about the rooms of Hull House led to interest in legislation that would protect them at their work. A representative of a manufacturers' association had the temerity to come to Jane Addams and offer her $50,000 to abandon a piece of legislation inimical to his interests. Needless to say, she did not take it.

And peace—among all the nations of the earth. That, perhaps equally with helping underprivileged neighbors, has been a crusade of Jane Addams' career. She hopes for a world completely without arms. She believes it will come. It will come by education. A great woman, with great ambitions for mankind. Lonely as a child. As a woman, one who has made Hull House, which is her home, the meeting place for all the lonely people of the world.

SUSAN B. ANTHONY

*Suffrage Banner Raised High
by Hand of Susan B. Anthony*

THE family which produced Susan Brownell Anthony had a reputation for rearing strong-minded women who were not afraid to face the public on issues they considered of importance.

Before Susan's day her father's mother had a "high seat" in Quaker meeting and his sister Hannah had been a Quaker preacher. Susan thus grew up in an atmosphere of independence and moral zeal.

Daniel Anthony set his daughters an example in unusual conduct for his day. He married a dancer. He was so opposed to slavery that he tried to get cotton for his mills which had not the taint of production by slave labor; he encouraged his daughters to find gainful occupation and he finally was read out of meeting for allowing the young people of the town to dance on the top floor of his house, instead of over the tavern, though his own children only "looked on."

Susan was precocious. She learned to read and write when she was 3 years old; she had an unusual memory and was eager for knowledge. She was born in Adams, Mass., but the family moved to Battensville, N. Y., and she went to district school there; then her father set up a school for his own and neighboring children. There was a period for Susan at Deborah Moulson's female seminary near Philadelphia, and Susan was prepared to teach school; the best job she held of this kind was as head of the "female department" of the Canajoharie Academy.

In her younger years Susan Anthony was a straitlaced young woman, as revealed by her letters. She got after an uncle for drinking ale and wine at yearly meeting. She rebuked President Van Buren without much hesitation for going to the theater.

She tired of teaching school and in 1850 was back in her home; such men as Frederick Douglass, Channing, Pillsbury, Garrison and Phillips were gathering there; she became acquainted also with Lucy

Stone, Elizabeth Stanton, Lucretia Mott, Amelia Bloomer, and it was easy to see that she was going to acquire some important interest of the day, make it her own and go forward with it.

Her first public work was for temperance. In 1852 she went as a delegate to a meeting of the Sons of Temperance in Albany. Upon a motion she got up to speak. She was quickly told that "the sisters were not invited here to speak, but to listen and learn." Susan did not like that. She and her friends went off and formed a Woman's State Temperance Society of New York.

She went to one convention after another. When the men hoped she would be silent, she insisted on being heard. She took to going to teachers' conventions and advocating that women should have all the rights enjoyed by men. In 1857-58 she camped under a banner, "No Union With Slaveholders."

After the war she advocated Negro suffrage. As if this were not enough to make her an object of national curiosity, she took to certain dress reforms; when she gave them up it was not because the adopted style displeased her, but that audiences which she wished to listen to her looked at her clothes instead.

Perhaps no woman in the chronicle of pioneers lived a more personally embattled life than Susan Anthony. People hissed her and did everything to throw her off her chosen track. But she had an indomitable will and a conviction that her causes were right. So she would not be shaken.

She was not grim to look at; on the contrary the papers of the period when she was about 35 reported her as having "pleasing, rather pretty features, a decidedly expressive countenance, rich brown hair effectively and not at all elaborately arranged, neither too tall nor too short, neither too plump nor too thin; in brief, one of those *juste-milieu* persons, the perfection of common sense physically exhibited."

In later years her face took on a certain angular austerity. But she had led a bold, aggressive life. She expressed her views with great frankness and occasionally she matched epithets with her opponents. She took little part in the social complexity about her, reserving her fire for the one idea which had captured her; it was in 1872 that she made a test of the legality of woman suffrage under the Fourteenth Amendment.

She registered with 15 other women and voted at the November elections in the city of Rochester. Two weeks later she was arrested for violating the law. Her trial was postponed and she voted again four months later. She prepared for her jury trial by an intensive lecture tour, aimed to educate voters from among whom the jury would be chosen.

The judge directed a verdict of guilty, refusing to allow the jury to be polled. Miss Anthony was fined $100. She said she would never pay a dollar of it. She never did. She said frequently she "would ignore all law to help a slave; and also to protect an enslaved woman."

CLARA BARTON

American Red Cross Founded on Initiative of Clara Barton

THIRTY-TWO nations were ahead of the United States in allying themselves with the Red Cross and there never would have been an American Red Cross perhaps but for Clara Barton—little in stature but large in resolute courage and strength; a New Englander, born in Oxford, Mass., and descendant of Edward Barton who came from England to Salem in 1640.

She early showed that she had no taste for being second in any undertaking and she might have stuck to school teaching, in which she engaged when she was 15, but for the fact that the school authorities thought the school had better have a male principal and Miss Barton made it speedily clear that she did not fancy herself as subordinate to such a figure.

Concise action was evidently her bent, and she took the initiative in many phases of the activities about her. From her school teaching, which lasted 18 years, radiated an abundance of useful variations upon the fundamental theme of social service.

In 1854 she went to Washington and found a job in the Patent Office. In April, 1861, the Sixth Massachusetts Regiment arrived in the capital, and there was lots to be done; many of the men had lost their baggage, coming through Baltimore, and Miss Barton fell to and helped fill in the deficiencies.

After the Battle of Bull Run she heard almost unbelievable stories of conditions on the field, due to lack of supplies. She decided the easiest way to get supplies quickly was to tell people she needed them, so she hurried off and put an advertisement in the Worcester Spy, and such quantities of things poured in she set up a distributing agency. And at this juncture was the final mold of her career set.

In July, 1862, she got permission from Surgeon-General Hammond to go on transports for the purpose of distributing comforts and nursing the wounded. Except possibly for a short period she never had any official connection with the army.

She simply recognized a need, took stock of her capabilities to oversee the filling of it, and developed herself as a constantly broadening agency of mercy.

For four years after the war ended she hunted for missing soldiers. Some she found. Some could not be found. In 1869 she went abroad to rest, but there was no rest for her once she perceived the fact of the International Red Cross of Geneva. She stayed in Strasbourg, ostensibly resting, but she found destitute women and children needing help, and before she knew it she was at work again.

She went to Geneva and some officials there said to her, "Why does not the United States join the Red Cross?" and she said, "I don't know, I'm sure; I'll find out." She underwent periodic intervals of physical frailty, but she never meant to leave off the idea of establishing the Red Cross in the States. And here her childhood habit of getting her own way came to her help.

She tried to get President Hayes to help her revise the position taken in Secretary Seward's day, against joining. The President wouldn't. But President Garfield did, and on May 21, 1881, the National Society of the Red Cross was founded. Before President Garfield could actually recommend the adoption of the Geneva Convention he was assassinated, but President Arthur and Secretary Blaine obtained confirmation from Congress in March, 1882.

Clara Barton was not a reformer, as we understand the term. She saw places in the social fabric that needed correcting, she summoned her patriotism and philanthropy, initiative, inflexible will, tenacity of purpose and devotion to human welfare and saw that they were corrected.

CARRIE CHAPMAN CATT

*Suffrage and Outlawry of War
Share in Mrs. Catt's Career*

WHEN Carrie Chapman Catt was born, in 1859, people were just putting themselves to rights after a period of economic decline. The

Civil War came along and another recession followed, and Mrs. Catt looks back now and says, with a sort of gentle wonder, "I never lived among people who knew anything about prosperity until about the year 1912."

Then the World War came, and again in its wake a recession, and you find, in a woman who recalls "about nine prosperous years out of my 74," a woman with a philosophy which would be a very good thing for the world if it were in general use. A philosophy which tends, when people say "the times are . . ." thus and so, to find work to do and to do it, and thus use up a lot of time profitably that might otherwise be devoted to vain imaginings.

Carrie Chapman Catt stands forever in the popular thought as a militant suffragist. Odd; you can talk with her for a long time and think of any quantity of things to suppose her long before it occurs to you to think of her as "militant" anything. At any rate, it must be supposed that the appellation "militant" has attached itself to her in its nicest meaning. Vigorous, diligent, earnest, zestful. Militant, so long as it does not bring in an unhappy picture of an intolerant person, careering about on a mission without regard to the rights of anyone standing in the way.

Mrs. Catt is a picture now; a picture of a woman who has lived fully, seen her best hopes realized, seen the world on the way to realize others which ran them a close second. Seen men and women become more understanding of the verities of living, better able to practice them.

Her abundant interest in the Committee on the Cause and Cure of War is based on a single, simple concept. That war, as one of the lower and least intelligent activities of mankind, from the dawn of time, needs to be understood in order that a taste or even a willingness to engage in it may be healed.

"It takes a hundred years to change the public mind on a great question," Mrs. Catt believes. Thus it will be given few of us to see a change of idea inaugurated and carried to a successful conclusion in our time, and it becomes all the more a privilege to concentrate energy in the time we have.

It was inevitable that Mrs. Catt be included in the list of women leaders. When she and Mary Garrett Hay cast their ballots in November, 1920, they stood for the successful fruition of a great idea before all the world.

As greatness goes, so simplicity goes. Today in New Rochelle, N. Y., Mrs. Catt lives in a comfortable, white house, surrounded by books and flowers and the bright and comfortable material residue of a happy and serviceable career. She has one special library of books on war, and they have furnished her with the reason for incessant labors to end war between nations, as a means of settling dispute.

Such a job is a job of education. When people in general learn what poor business war is, war will be no more. It requires patience, to teach people such facts. And perhaps the one sentence that could accurately sum up Mrs. Catt's career and the things she has successfully done would be, "She is a patient woman."

MARY BAKER EDDY

*Religious Leader Won Place
by Revealing Healing Truth*

by ANNIE M. KNOTT

It has probably come as a surprise to newspaper readers that Mrs. Eddy's name should head the list of the 12 great women leaders in the United States during the last 100 years. It may be said that she was born in New England, July 16, 1821; she was reared among deeply religious and thoughtful people, and from her earliest days was a profound thinker.

As to Mrs. Eddy's personal appearance when she was actively engaged in the work of the Massachusetts Metaphysical College in the '80s, it may be said that it was remarkable. Her hair was abundant and beautiful, of a rich brown color, while her complexion was as fresh as that of a woman of 25, and her figure erect and graceful.

It would have been extremely difficult to have guessed her age at this period, as there was a freshness not always seen even in very young persons, but there was also a sort of mental maturity to which few people attain, and that spiritual poise which is not swayed by the passing of the years, but which betokens a reflection of the changeless life of Spirit.

We have St. Paul's word for it, that, when the veil of material sense is taken away, those who behold the glory of the Lord "are changed into the same likeness"; and while the primary signification of this likeness is undoubtedly that of mind and character, it can also be expressed by the face, as in the case of Moses, when he caught foregleams of man's immortality in the holy mount.

Of Mary Baker Eddy much has been written by both friends and foes; in all cases because she is known throughout the world as the Discoverer and Founder of Christian Science, and the author of its textbook "Science and Health with Key to the Scriptures." This statement doubtless means to many that Mrs. Eddy has founded a new religion known as Christian Science. To those, however, who have proved its efficacy in overcoming disease with its attendant suffering and fear, Mrs. Eddy's gift to humanity means the restoration of the Christ-healing brought to the world through Jesus of Nazareth, and simply yet impressively recorded in the Bible.

Some years ago there were those who objected to the term "Science" in connection with religion, yet it should be remembered that about the time when Mrs. Eddy was endeavoring to prove to herself and others that the healing work of Christ Jesus expressed law and order, physical science was endeavoring to explain as never before the meaning of life and law.

Mrs. Eddy's teachings from the first dealt with the true idea of God and man, of Life and Truth. At that day some of the most advanced thinkers did not hesitate to say that life was unknown. Some ventured to say that electricity might be life, yet from this viewpoint the moral and intellectual element was lacking. Mrs. Eddy, however, did not hesitate to declare that God is the life and intelligence of man and the universe.

Here we may recall St. Paul's words as found in his Epistle to the Romans,—"For the law of the spirit of life in Christ Jesus hath made me free from the law of sin and death," or, to state it otherwise, we find the supposed law of sin and death annulled by "the law of the spirit of life in Christ Jesus."

At this point it may be argued that the Christian world in general was supposed to accept unquestioningly the authority of this very definite statement of Scripture, but the fact is that the application of the truth as here stated was questioned by many and the availability of this truth in time of human need doubted and even denied by professing Christians. In the present writer's experience a gleam of light came from a sermon preached by an eloquent and distinguished clergyman, his text being from the sixty-eighth Psalm: "He that is our God is the God of salvation; and unto God the Lord belong the issues from death."

Encouraged by this sermon to look to God as never before for help in the overcoming of illness where material means were proved of no avail, the well-known preacher was appealed to by letter, but replied promptly saying that it was a mistake to ask a clergyman to heal a sick person when it was self-evident that all such cases should be cared for by the medical profession. Had the recipient of this letter not seen a ray of light before this time, the preacher's response would have made of her an atheist, especially as this experience was followed by several others of similar character with clergymen of different denominations.

When Mrs. Eddy began to tell the world that the healing work practiced and taught by Christ Jesus was clearly meant by him to continue throughout the ages, not many were ready to pause long enough to give this the consideration it deserved, yet it was an era when new ideals were receiving much attention.

In England Methodism had called many away from the state church, and in America Universalism and Unitarianism were drawing to their communion many thoughtful and spiritually minded people. Throughout the centuries since the days of Christ Jesus and his followers there had been many godly men and women who had had experiences in the healing of disease, but apparently none had come to think of it as an essential and inseparable element of Christianity.

The world was undoubtedly better for the Christian men and women who had helped to keep the light of Truth burning even though dimly, yet the centuries waited for the understanding of the divine Principle and law of the Christ-healing, waited for someone who was ready to prove what the Christ-healing can do in any age.

Here it may be well to quote from the textbook, Science and Health (295:19-24), "The mortal mind through which Truth appears most vividly is that one which has lost much materiality—much error—in order to become a better transparency for Truth. Then, like a cloud melting into thin vapor, it no longer hides the sun." This explains in large measure Mrs. Eddy's place as a great spiritual leader.

Those who had the privilege of studying with Mrs. Eddy did not find it difficult to believe what is recorded in the Bible as to the healing work of Christ Jesus and his disciples, and never was their credulity taxed by the inconsistent statement that what was once true is so no longer. No! It was unchanging divine Principle and law, the light growing clearer as material belief gave place to spiritual Truth.

A man who had never been interested in religion awakened to his need of it when a member of his family was given up by physicians to die. The sick man was, however, healed through Christian Science and became Mrs. Eddy's student. His father said to the present writer he was then sure that God is, and is available in all our need. He, too, became Mrs. Eddy's student and had remarkable experiences in the healing ministry of Christian Science. He said that he could never doubt the Scripture record of Jesus' work because in his humble way he, himself, was proving daily and hourly that the Master's teaching is applicable in the overcoming of all that is unlike God.

Inseparably connected with the healing work of Christian Science is The Mother Church and its branches the world over, for each one of these announces to all mankind that the Christ-healing is as truly with us today as when Christ Jesus declared (always in the future tense) that the "Comforter," the "Spirit of truth," would come and bring all things to our remembrance, whatsoever he had said to his disciples. The textbook of Christian Science is indeed a "Key to the Scriptures" and enables its students to demonstrate the truth of the inspired word rather than to interpret it, and this is proved by them in all their undertakings. The Master himself said: "If I do not the works of my Father, believe me not. But if I do, though ye believe not me, believe the works."

Some of those who were privileged in being taught by Mrs. Eddy went out from her classes and had results in healing which surprised and awed themselves. The world was then slowly awakening to the meaning of Paul's words, "Christ in you, the hope of glory." Now humanity is more nearly awake, and the 11 women whose names are associated with that of Mrs. Eddy, as leaders in the United States during the past 100 years, have had their share in this awakening. Furthermore, all faithful students of Christian Science can prove for themselves in their healing work that Mrs. Eddy was divinely inspired to lay hold anew upon the closing words of the First Gospel, "Go ye therefore, and teach all nations . . . teaching them to observe all things whatsoever I have commanded you." "Heal the sick!"

JULIA WARD HOWE

Melodious Hymn of Patriotism
Enriched Fame of Suffragist

Woman suffrage was a part with patriotism, in the heart of Julia Ward Howe. And, having seen something of the Civil War, the cause of international peace, as she believed it could be developed, was always in her thought as well.

Julia Ward was born in New York City, of the line that included Roger Williams, the founder of Rhode Island. By the time she was 17, Julia Ward, whose home surroundings were cultured and intellectually vigorous, was writing for magazines. She knew a variety of languages; she took care to be well informed; she married; she went to Boston to live. And there her drawing room became a center of the social and intellectual life of the city.

In literature she was commonly classified as a prose writer. But she wrote a poem, as most prose writers do at one time and another, and that poem was "The Battle Hymn of the Republic," which was to do more for her enduring fame than all her other writings together.

In its way, the poem was the reply of cultured woman to vulgarity. In war-time Washington she had seen men marching along the streets, their boots beating time on the road to "John Brown's Body"; and she listened, and the words distressed her, and she thought that there might be another such song, of sharp rhythm and persuasive melody, and that its words might be ennobling instead of cheap. She thought some about it, and tucked the idea in the back of her thought. One night she woke up and a more complete thought came to her on the subject; and she lighted a lamp, and found a pen and some scraps of paper and wrote quickly.

After she had gone back to sleep, and waked again, it was hard for her to make out what she had written. But she puzzled over it, and retraced her thought and re-ordered what she had written, and the poem was printed in the Atlantic Monthly in February, 1862. And the thing which really pleased Mrs. Howe was that the soldiers liked the words and quickly adopted them for a marching song.

Many honors were showered on Julia Ward Howe. And the one which touched her most was the one which summed up the whole Julia Ward Howe. It was given her by Smith College in 1910, and she wore a soft white dress, with a black silk academic gown over it and she did not think it necessary to take off her customary white lace cap before she put on the accompanying mortar board and her name was the last to be reached, for the bestowal of honors. And 2000 girls who were there, also in white dresses, heard the organ peal in signal, and stood and sang "Mine eyes have seen the glory of the coming of the Lord . . ."

And Julia Ward Howe's cup was even then full and running over and the citation of the degree was the last benison of a full life. And it began, "Julia Ward Howe, poet and patriot, lover of letters and learning, advocate for over half a century, in print and living speech, of great causes of human liberty, sincere friend of all that makes for the elevation and enrichment of womanhood. . . ."

HELEN KELLER

Milestones of Unselfish Service
Chart Pathway of Helen Keller

Now or at any later time, the simplest and most accurate thing that can be said of Helen Keller is "She made herself useful."

A splendid example of a complete triumph over an infirmity, Miss Keller's career has been a series of tableaus of progress. From one stage to another she has gone with vigor and good humor. Those who know her well and see her often, say of her that she is one of the happiest individuals in the world—with the kind of happiness which comes from putting self aside, and laboring to accomplish good for others.

Helen Keller was born in Tuscumbia, Ala., the daughter of a landpoor southerner of colonial lineage, and until she was seven her world seemed to those at hand to hold little promise for her.

But there then crossed her path Miss Anne Mansfield Sullivan, a young school-teacher, to whom somehow the vision was given that here was a life that need not be spoiled because of a physical handicap.

By slow, careful beginnings, a system of teaching was begun. With what success these beginnings were crowned it is only necessary to say that in 1904 Miss Keller was graduated with honors.

By 1918, Miss Sullivan, now Mrs. Macy, and an additional secretary, Miss Polly Thompson, were living in a household together at Forest Hills on Long Island, a household busy with constructive plans for bringing persons handicapped as Miss Keller had been into a heritage of usefulness and happiness.

Lectures and stage appearances have kept Helen Keller before the world; not for personal aggrandizement but all to the end that she might help others. The widening use of Braille books and making them available to those who could not afford to buy them for themselves; the establishment of scholarships for ambitious, handicapped boys and girls; the spreading of knowledge which would make possible and encourage the participation of friends all over the world in the problem of smoothing away that seemed hard for underprivileged people—these have been her contributions to progress.

She has been greatly honored. When the honors have carried with them awards of money Miss Keller has made haste to turn them into funds for her interesting and important projects. When she might have been thought to live in a world of considerable solitude, she has said the exact opposite was true; she has savored the amusements and interests of her fellows, ridden in airplanes, gone on camping trips, sat in a motion picture house beside Charles Chaplin, visited houses of royalty in Europe, climbed mountains, sailed great rivers and oceans, owned pets, loved the rush and roar of great cities, and the peace and quiet of the country.

When she could easily have been a stone the builders of the world would have rejected, she has made herself a stone of utmost importance, pointing the way to others who have followed her example in carrying through the great and kindly things that a world, made thoughtful, may do for those unable to do them for themselves.

MARY LYON

*Quality of Durability Places Educator
in Hall of Fame*

WHEN Mary Lyon managed, after many discouragements and delays, to open a seminary for girls in South Hadley, Mass., she called it the Mount Holyoke Female Seminary. Those were purist days and the 80 pupils were not young ladies, or even young women; they were females with a thirst for education.

Like many of her class, Mary Lyon gave early promise of engaging in the field of education. She became a teacher when she was 18 and she was associate principal of a Female Academy at Londonderry, N. H., for a time. She was born in Buckland, Mass., in February of 1797 and she felt there was a place for women in the world outside the home—though their talents would necessarily find expression in some phase that supplemented the life of the home—and that place would probably be the field of education.

Mary Lyon felt that she was a teacher who had deficiencies, and she wanted to educate other young women away from deficiency. Then, too, she had a period of association with a clergyman, the Rev. Joseph Emerson of Newburyport, and she got herself talked about for concurring with him in a belief that women, whether they intended to become teachers or not, ought to be able to enjoy equal educational advantages with men. "Outlandish!" cried observers, but Mary Lyon, remembering her own slim educational chances, said, "Nothing of the kind!" and went resolutely about her plans.

It was hard in those days to find backing for the establishment of a Seminary for Girls—even a seminary which it was purposed to make one big family, in which study would be systematic and a full life of social adjustment to the group lived. Malice, ridicule and disapproval eddied about the determined head of Mary Lyon. When she asked some people for money, they laughed at her. Eighteen hundred other persons, scattered about in 91 towns, gave her $27,000, in sums which ranged from two gifts respectively of three and six cents, to two proud gifts of $1000 each.

When the corner stone was laid for the seminary which opened November 8, 1837, Mary Lyon said, "The stones, brick and mortar speak a language which vibrates through my very soul."

Mount Holyoke College has come a long way since the days of Mary Lyon, when two of the important rules were that every student must walk a mile a day, and must bring with her to the seminary, clothes to be worn in inclement weather.

Mary Lyon lived 12 years after her seminary was established. She had the joy of seeing it take root. She must have smiled when she heard it commented upon as "one of the most astonishing experiments in radical democracy; radical because it is an institution for women; democratic because Miss Lyon, who goes about collecting pennies, nickels and dimes, which she puts in a green bag—has made thousands of New Englanders partners in her great forward-looking enterprise."

But the quality that brings Mary Lyon now to this company in the Hall of Fame is durability. She wore well, when her ideas were tested. Laughter, suspicion, the insistent clamor of lazy tongues, these she could ignore; because of a wistful yearning of her own when she was young, that she had had a better schooling; and an indomitable determination, now that she was grown, to make it possible for others to have what was established too late for her to participate in as a pupil.

AMELIA EARHART PUTNAM

*Zest for Trying New Things Inspired Deeds
of Woman Flier*

When thought is taken of what is called courage as shown by Amelia Earhart, it ought not to be lightly passed over as something which comes without a struggle.

Whistling to keep up one's courage is a familiar device and Miss Earhart's early days of flight were not without their meed of this practical self-service. The first time she "soloed," and that would have been in California, she went up 5000 feet and she says now she can only remember that she sang, in an indifferent voice but definitely loudly, and that very possibly what would have struck observers, if there had been any at hand to receive full advantage of the spectacle, as odd at the least was very likely an actual help in the circumstances.

The last thing in the world that Amelia Earhart gave definite promise of when she was a little girl was of becoming the first woman to fly the Atlantic Ocean solo.

She wasn't mechanical, unless you can count a shrewd device she fashioned for impeding neighbors' chickens, when they wandered into her yard.

Still, there were one or two threads. Her father was a railroad man and sometimes he took Amelia with him on trips. That fixed a liking for movement, for seeing new places and new people. Joined to that was a certain streak which inspired her to try new things.

She was born in Atchison, Kan. Skipping back two generations and Quakers are found contributing to her make-up. A Quaker grandmother went west, under stress of family circumstances, and Kansas was still quite wild; men were shoving aside piles of buffalo bones so they could lay railroad tracks, and Indians shuffled about.

The Indians and the buffaloes were definitely of the past before Amelia Earhart became acquainted with Kansas. Still, there was a flavor. . . .

She read a lot. Her childhood was still a period when girls were supposed to remain, definitely girls. She played games outdoors that people felt uneasily belonged to boys. Not with particular skill or grace, but with immense zest. She first rode horseback, not on a saddle horse but on the back of a delivery horse, fully and solidly hitched to the delivery cart. The shafts and the trundling wagon were not what she would have wished, but they were there, inevitable in the situation, and better to put up with them than miss the ride.

Her thought was shaping, and in it there was noticeable a strong tendency to inquire "What's over there, just out of sight?"

And to go and try to find out.

She got out of high school and went on a visit to Toronto. She realized what a World War means. She got a job in a hospital.

In the winter of 1918 she discovered airplanes, as something within reach of the comprehension of such as she.

Her sister was in college in Northampton, and Amelia beguiled some time taking a course in automobile engine repair.

She was in California. She and her father visited a flying field. She forced her father to obtain an academic opinion as to how long it takes a person to learn to fly, and how much it cost—then.

Her father said, "Why do you want to know?" and found out for her, and failed to see in his daughter's face a conviction that she would presently apply the information.

She stole off by herself and "bought a hop." The ship took off from a rather sketchy field surrounded by oil wells. The pilot was Frank Hawks. That means something now. It didn't, then. When the ship left the ground Amelia Earhart knew she was going to be a flier. How, when, what did it matter?

It wasn't easy. Nothing is easy that amounts to anything.

All that was quite a time ago. She has made many records. Best of all, she has made a record of her type. A sane, balanced, quiet, organized girl, capable of vision, capable of putting the vision into action. People who have known her a long time say, "She hasn't changed." She never shows excitement. She never lifts her voice to a clatter. Her touch is sure, and light.

She says the transatlantic flight alone did not take courage. She thinks of courage as an effort against oneself. The flight wasn't against herself. It was the thing she wanted most to do. She waited to do it until she thought she was ready. And then did it.

HARRIET BEECHER STOWE

Power of "Uncle Tom's Cabin" Won Author World Renown

Harriet beecher stowe was the daughter of a woman who expected all her sons to become ministers. And, so long as there was a daughter, it seemed best that she should have the same kind of an education.

But Lyman Beecher's daughter did not want to stop at prescribed reading for the ministry. So she read everything she could lay her hands on. Sometimes she had to be careful about it. Her mother would not have cared to see her reading "The Arabian Nights," for instance. But there were not many such outbreaks, and when she married, Harriet Beecher married a Professor Stowe, who taught sacred literature in a theological seminary.

Harriet Stowe was born June 14, 1811, in Litchfield, Conn. A historian has said. "The family home was a nest of geniuses." Seven sons became ministers, according to their mother's plan. There were other daughters, with vigorous, ambitious individualities, but it was left for Harriet to write a book which was that interesting thing of its time, "fiction, with a didactic purpose."

The Beecher house must sometimes almost have burst with the energy exhibited by its young people in their various cultural developments. The boys were reading Latin grammar at 7 or 8 years, and had a full and happy expectation of reading "Paradise Lost," when they were 12. It was a popular "mot" of the day to say that "The human race is divided into saints, sinners and the Beecher family."

Yet prolific in literature as the sons and daughters were, in the benign and busy shadow of their great father, it is a curious fact that little of their writings remain to be particularly noted outside of "Uncle Tom's Cabin."

There were not so many "reforms" flying through the air in the middle years of the last century as there are today, and now, with all the more material, where can be found either a man or woman writing fiction which deals with social

[42]

issues in equal graphic power, moral passion and ability to appraise and state a popular feeling as "Uncle Tom's Cabin" did?

"Uncle Tom's Cabin" appeared in the National Era, a weekly paper, printed in Washington in June, 1851. And it attracted no particular attention at the time.

But the minute a Boston publisher brought it out in book form things began to happen. It sold 300,000 copies in the United States the first year, a sale equivalent to 1,500,000 nowadays. England fell upon it with interest, and France as well. All the more important languages were used for its translation, and some obscure tongues as well.

It did immeasurable good in a living cause, and it provided one of the literary phenomena of all time. It wasn't a very good book, from a literary standpoint, but it was a powerful polemic and it came to be as much a part of the abolition of slavery as the Civil War or the Emancipation Proclamation.

And it lasted. It is not a dull book today, out of its time though it is. No one can read it today, or tomorrow, or 100 years from now, without feeling that the sympathies stirred by the cause of the slave are one with those that forever move the world of good men and women in their efforts to right the wrongs of the political and social system.

FRANCES E. WILLARD

*Goal of Total Abstinence Set to World
by Frances Willard*

FRANCES E. WILLARD was one of the first internationalists among women. In 1884 she founded the World Woman's Christian Temperance Union and called upon women the world over "to protect

[44]

the home, outlaw the liquor traffic, seek and procure enfranchisement of women, work to establish courts of international arbitration, demand an equal standard of purity for men and women and labor unceasingly that justice may be opposed to greed and gain, and that Christ's Golden Rule may triumph, in custom and in law."

Born in Churchville, N. Y., in September, 1849, Miss Willard was a direct descendant of the Simon Willard who left Horsmonden in Kent, Eng., in 1634, and became a founder of Concord, Mass., in the new world.

In February of last year a scrapbook was discovered in the attic of Rest Cottage, where Miss Willard lived at Evanston, Ill., for many years, and in that scrapbook the great pioneer of philanthropy and reform had gathered materials which threw a bright and satisfying light upon the progress made from little beginnings nearly a half century before, when the National Council of Women was founded to band together into an increasing force to bring about those elements of betterment the world lacked.

They were a capable lot, those women who met for the first time in 1888. Among them were Susan B. Anthony, Julia Ward Howe, Clara Barton, Lucy Stone, Elizabeth Cady Stanton and others. While the first inclination of some of the Washington newspapers of the day was to laugh at the spectacle of these earnest women who had come out of their homes, leaving pots and kettles and kitchens and nurseries, commonly counted their "proper domain," to engage in discussion about world affairs, gradually the papers took the delegates more seriously, in proportion as the reporters observed the earnestness and capability with which the women set to work on the job they saw to be done.

In 44 years the National Council of Women has grown to 5,000,000 through affiliated groups and out of plans laid at that first meeting there grew an International Council of Women, with affiliated councils in 43 countries.

A country woman, Miss Willard went to school in a little frame building two miles southwest of Janesville, Wis., near Rock River. Her father and some of the husbandmen of the district built the school, and when Miss Willard was older she went back and taught in the same room where she had bent her pigtailed head over a little wooden desk.

Frances Willard is the only woman represented in the Statuary Hall of the Capitol at Washington. She early caught a vision of a regenerated world. She believed total abstinence was one virtue that would not only revive a disappointed and disappointing world but open a vast vista of improvement in child welfare, legislation, world peace and all the aspects of the communal life of the world.

Although she managed to average speaking at not less than one meeting a day and sometimes more for a period of 10 years, Miss Willard also managed to sandwich in a period of newspaper work; she was editor of the Chicago Post and Mail for a short time after 1878, experience which stood her in good stead when for six years she was editor of the Union Signal, the official organ of the temperance movement.

MARY EMMA WOOLLEY

Arts of Education and Peace Fill Days for Miss Woolley

CONNECTICUT born, New England by education, New England by the outstanding administration of a great college for women, Mary Emma Woolley gives to the list of women leaders a striking example of the liberal viewpoint with particular application to matters of peace among nations. In 1931 she was appointed by President Hoover to be the first woman delegate to an international conference on disarmament.

Dr. Woolley has been president of Mount Holyoke for 32 years and it must, in some ways, have been a wrench for her to leave the institution whose career is her career even for the comparatively short period of the conference. But feeling that the education of youth is inextricably woven with a growing appreciation for and participation in an attitude of world peace and understanding, she accepted the appointment and no one who has heard her speak since she came back from Geneva can doubt that her educational viewpoint has been enriched and made more fruitful by the great experience of Geneva.

Mary Woolley was born in Norwalk, Conn., in 1863, the daughter of a clergyman, the Rev. Joseph J., and Mary A. (Ferris) Woolley. In 1894 she received the first bachelor's degree ever awarded a woman by Brown University. In 1895 she received a master's degree at the same university and in 1900 Brown gave her an LL. D.

She was "cut out" for a teacher, as they say, and she began teaching at Wheaton, then Wheaton Seminary, just before the turn of the century. And although there have been youthful college presidents in later years, the appointment of Miss Woolley to the presidency of Mount Holyoke in 1900, when she was only 37, astonished the educational world.

A sturdy block of woman is Miss Woolley, with a squarish, vigorous figure, and fine, alert eyes and glossy brown hair, done with a New England-ish air. Her voice is strong and reedy, and once you have heard it you are not likely to forget it, any more than Miss Woolley is likely to forget your face once she has seen you, or the little odds and ends she has managed to learn about you in a surprisingly short time.

She likes to talk peace. She believes in peace for the world. She believes war is a pit out of which it is difficult for nations that have engaged in it ever to climb.

It is probable that when there was a war she did her part in the grim things it was necessary to do; but when the war was over, and people had a chance to sit down and think about it, she came to the conclusion that it is desirable to cultivate a spirit of mercy rather than of cruelty, to the end that the quality of mercy may not have to be tried on battlefields, and that it is infinitely preferable to exalt the virtue of reason rather than of violence, and that there are splendors of peace which far exceed the splendors of war and that those who substitute in their hearts international understanding and a willingness to arbitrate for the panoply of armed force will not be the losers.

In "The President's House" at South Hadley Miss Woolley lives a rich life; bird houses are hung in her trees; collie dogs fly in a blur of white and gold in and out of the house. Friends come and go. There is an air of business; good business, having to do with the progress of men toward better things.

And at the college there are twice as many students to be looked out for as there were when Miss Woolley took over in 1900, and nearly six times as many faculty members, and any number of new buildings and an opportunity as wide as the world. Opportunity which even a freshman would tell you Miss Woolley makes haste to seize.

PRIZE ESSAYS
ON "THE ESSENTIAL QUALITIES OF A WOMAN LEADER"

A woman with a lamp shall stand in the history of the land . . a noble type . . of good, heroic womanhood. — Longfellow

From the several thousand essays entered in The Ladies' Home Journal's contest on the "Essential Qualities of Women Leadership," these five were selected by the judges to receive the awards. The judges appointed by the National Council of Women were Ida Tarbell, Maud Wood Park and Dr. Mary Woolley.

However, it seems apropos to comment upon the other essays which were received, for all were worthy of consideration.

Constantly repeated through these essays was that verse of Longfellow placed upon this page. And it seemed that every woman was measuring herself while writing of feminine leadership; that every woman had, by focusing her thought upon this fascinating subject, visualized herself as a leader in whatever phase of life and opportunity was hers.

The six qualities most frequently mentioned in a hundred of these essays were courage, love and understanding of humanity, self-sacrifice, sincerity and tenacity of purpose, personality and vision. These are the six primary qualities which women look for in their leaders and by which they strive to practice their leadership.

Reprinted by permission from
The Ladies' Home Journal, April, 1933

THESE PRIZES WERE AWARDED

$100.00 *for the best 300 word letter*
50.00 *for the second prize*
*10.00 *for the third prize*
5.00 *for fourth prize*
Two awards made for third prize.

FIRST PRIZE ESSAY
by REBECCA F. GROSS

Essentials of leadership are: The vision to discover an avenue of progress, the courage to explore it with determination and devotion, and the magnetism to draw others along the same path toward a goal whose achievement will bring benefits to more than a select, restricted group of human beings.

Unless she knows her objective and can chart a path that leads to it, a woman is no leader; unless she can marshal her forces for a practical and effective program, ignoring none of the possibilities for presenting the merits of her cause, refusing to let her efforts flag in the face of obstacles and discouragement, her work will be weak; and unless she can impress her aims upon enough others so that her cause can command a hearing among the conflicting interests and cross-purposes of the world of affairs, she will fail in the ultimate aim of leadership.

A true leader is not animated by selfish motives. She is one who recognizes the public and general good above personal interest or the interests of a small group, and one who labors with greater zeal in the more disinterested cause. To lead effectively, she must comprehend human nature and understand modern social, industrial and economic machinery, and her knowledge of the special field she has chosen for her own must be that of an expert. Without such equipment her leadership cannot receive respect from her followers or her critics.

The woman leader must rise above the common stature, in spiritual, mental and moral qualities; she must inspire, convince and sustain, not only her followers but herself. She dare not be a fanatic in her own devotion to her aims, nor a sycophant in her endeavors to win a following. She must be able to discount flattery and praise and equally to weather disappointment and criticism.

Above all, the woman who leads must keep alive her sense of human values, her sense of proportion, and her belief that men and women who work unselfishly to create a better world do not do so in vain.

SECOND PRIZE ESSAY
by EDITH COLEMAN

THAT rare quality of leadership—what is it, indeed? Not a keen mind, nor a facile pen, nor a divine voice, unless that mind or that pen or that voice translate itself into the everyday lives of other women and enable them to more nearly fulfill their possibilities as women.

True leadership must always mean helping others to help themselves. This essential of leadership may assert itself in home life, in community activities or in the larger vistas of national and international relationships. Subhead under it, if you will, courage, unselfishness, enthusiasm, vision, tact and the rest. The real test of a woman's contribution to human progress is not what she has said or done for her family or community or country, but what that family or community or country is then able to do for itself.

This may merely mean helping an individual to a happier adjustment to his surroundings at home or in school or in business. It may mean only that five or six middle-aged women have, through her, found an outlet for the urge within them in creative writing. It may mean that through her influence her women's club has achieved a constructive program for the welfare of the underprivileged and mal-adjusted children in their schools. Perhaps she is a woman judge, through whose court pass countless women and girls yearly, and whose opportunity it is to send them out into more normal lives. Maybe she envisages world peace and helps her sister world citizens work out a practical gospel for peace which women may promote in their own lands.

This, then, I hold to be the criterion, not of greatness but of leadership, great or small—helping other women to enrich their own lives and the lives of those about them.

THIRD PRIZE ESSAY
by ELEANOR LINTON

To be a Leader, a woman must possess and cultivate the basic qualities of integrity, creative imagination and social consciousness.

Integrity is the bedrock of all greatness. No woman can permanently influence the lives of others who has not first herself come to terms sincerely and effectively with the problems of her own life and recognized her motives, aspirations and limitations. She must be loyal to the laws of her own soul and not a blind follower of tradition or collective opinion. The truth, as it emerges from within, must be her lodestar.

Only the person who lives undauntedly true to her belief is trustworthy as a leader. The greatest personal magnetism, indeed, is but the flame of inner probity which kindles and gleams through minor attributes and without which they fall short, however brilliant or endearing.

The woman leader must have creative imagination to organize the people interested in a common cause, or to add her bit to scientific, philosophic or artistic progress. Often she does both, for though generally the student becomes the originator and the humanitarian the organizer, there must always be some of both in each. Creative imagination sometimes bursts through ordinary human trappings in sparks of genius, but chiefly it entails struggle, labor and grueling persistence.

The mantle of leadership falls finally only on the woman who is clear in her relationships to her fellow men. She must reckon patiently with human idiosyncrasies, and take up the cudgels for her own convictions without the taint of coercion or small personal ends. She must be socially minded in a cosmic as well as an immediate sense, for whether her life interest is science, art or welfare, her contribution will be significant only as she measures by enduring universal values.

THIRD PRIZE ESSAY
(Two awards made for third prize)
by KATHARINE B. MEIGS

WHEN I came to consider what women I thought should be named on the National Council List, I wished with all my heart there could be an entry called "The Unknown Woman."

For in this country today there are, unheralded and unsung, hundreds and thousands of women whose individual achievements, right in their own homes, deserve recognition and praise.

My "Unknown Woman" is the woman whose entire domestic life has been re-created to meet the present economic conditions. She is the wife of a salaried man whose income, only a few years ago, allowed them a comfortable living, with the luxury, perhaps, of cars and servants. She herself had her pleasures and amusements, besides her charitable interests; her children were in private schools; and life was serene and perhaps luxurious, surely secure.

Today, that woman is confronted with a tremendous task that requires tact, courage and initiative. On her rely her family, the important unit of our civilization. On her individual leadership depends the making or breaking of her family, and it is for that woman, in grave financial difficulties, that I want to vote.

For she is confronted with the task of reconstructing her life and theirs on a new plane. The family income, in her case, has shrunk at least 75 per cent, and she faces the fear and terror of having her husband lose even his job. In spite of this precarious outlook, she must face the future without complaint. Her husband's and children's morale must not suffer any more than their physical welfare must. Her house must be kept in order in every respect, and though she is cook, housemaid, nurse and chauffeur, she must still take time to be well groomed and outwardly calm.

She has no time to be ill and no money for new clothes. She keeps her children looking fresh and neat and wears her old clothes with nonchalance, and she resents sympathy for her new rôle and discourages the complaints of others. Her neighbors respect and admire her, and her husband's appreciation is beyond words.

She is a gallant soldier in the battle of life, concealing her wounds and fighting to the finish. She will never get any medals; and though she shows courage equal to that of pioneer women, she will probably get no recognition.

And though her candle sheds only a little light, thank God

there are thousands of American women like her to illuminate the dark places in our hearts today.

To that "Unknown Woman" leader of families and friends, my twelfth vote.

FOURTH PRIZE ESSAY
by RUTH NEES

FIRST of all, the woman leader has vision. She sees a future more nearly perfect because of some wrong righted, some greater justice done. She catches the gleam, and pulls back the curtains of ignorance and indifference so that others, too, may see and follow.

But she possesses more than the dreams of an idealist. She has *initiative*. She not only sees the need for action; she acts.

She has *faith*—in her cause and her followers, in her country and her God.

She has *courage*, a courage backed by the strength of conviction, a courage that faces and conquers the obstacles of thoughtlessness, disbelief and outright antagonism.

She has *loyalty*. She is loyal to her ideas, to her ideals and to humanity. Her loyalty is such that she is willing to give the last full measure of devotion.

She is *intelligent*. With a mind capable of directing her desire for service into workable ideas, with the ability to devise and carry out efficient plans, she has the wisdom of an understanding heart.

Leadership necessarily implies followers. And to have followers, not only the cause must have an appeal to the people, but the leader must have a *personality* capable of attracting followers and holding them. This, of course, includes tact, sympathy, patience and power.

However, with all these qualities, the woman leader is not a goddess but a woman, with the qualities that abide in the hearts of all women—intensified, perhaps, and combined with a burning, unresting zeal. And of all the qualities that lie in the hearts of womankind, the greatest is *love*. And it is this deep, abiding love, transformed into service, that is the most essential quality of the woman leader.